Look Up

WELDON OWEN PTY LTD

Publisher: Sheena Coupe
Senior Designer: Kylie Mulquin
Editorial Coordinators: Sarah Anderson,
Tracey Gibson
Production Manager: Helen Creeke
Production Assistant: Kylie Lawson

Project Editor: Ariana Klepac
Designer: Patricia Ansell
Text: Jan Stradling

05 04 03 02
10 9 8 7 6 5 4 3 2

Published in New Zealand by
Shortland Publications,
10 Cawley Street, Ellerslie, Auckland.
Published in the United Kingdom by
Kingscourt/McGraw-Hill,
Shoppenhangers Road, Maidenhead,
Berkshire, SL6 2QL.
Published in Australia by **Mimosa Shortland**,
8 Yarra Street, Hawthorn, Victoria 3122.

Printed in Singapore
ISBN: 0-7699-1253-2

CREDITS AND ACKNOWLEDGMENTS

PICTURE AND ILLUSTRATION CREDITS
[t=top, b=bottom, l=left, r=right, c=centre]
Mike Atkinson/ Garden Studio (now called illustration) 6b. **Barry Croucher** 7b. **Akira Fujii** 14b. **Corel Corp.** banding, 4b, 5t, 5bl, 10tr, 12tr, 12tl, 16bc. **Digital Stock** 3b, 8b, 9br. **Mike Gorman** 11. **Ray Grinaway** (J. Brackenbury/ Cassell) 3t, 6c. **David Hardy/Wildlife Art Ltd.** 13, 14–15. **Rob Mancini** 1, 7tl. **Photodisc** 7cr, 9cr. **Jonathon Potter/Wildlife Art Ltd.** 12b. **Ray Sim** 10b. **Rod Westblade** 9l.

Weldon Owen would like to thank the following people for their assistance in the production of this book:
Peta Gorman, Michael Hann, Marney Richardson.

Contents

Daytime

When we look up at the sky in the daytime we can see the Sun. Sometimes clouds cover the Sun but it is always shining.

Sunsets can be very colourful.

Sometimes when it is raining and the Sun is shining we can see a rainbow.

Flying By

When we look up we can see birds and insects flying in the air. They are all around us.

Butterfly

Dragonfly

Blue jay

Plant seeds
float in
the air too.

Crows

Up in the Clouds

There are different types of clouds. Cumulus clouds are white and puffy. Stratus clouds are long and thin. Cirrus clouds are thin and wispy.

Cumulus clouds

Cirrus clouds tell us
strong winds
are coming.

Types of clouds

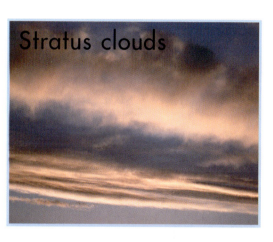

Stratus clouds

Cumulonimbus
clouds often bring
thunder, lightning
and rain storms.

Cirrus clouds

Stratus are
rain clouds.

Cumulus are
fine weather
clouds.

There is a lot happening in the sky. Skies can be stormy or clear.
Clouds make lightning, rain, hail and snow.

Types of lightning

Cloud to ground   Cloud to cloud   Inside a cloud

Rain   Hail   Snow

Nighttime

At nighttime we can see stars. They look like lights in the night sky. We can see the Moon too.

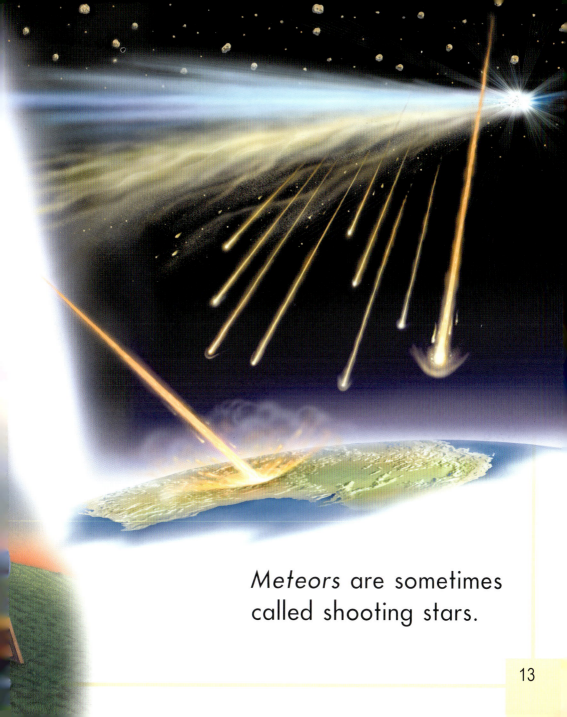

Meteors are sometimes called shooting stars.

Out in Space

Neptune

Pluto

Earth is a *planet*. Sometimes we can see other planets in the night sky. We can see these clearly if we look through a *telescope*.

Did You Know?

The rings of Saturn were first seen by a scientist using a small telescope.

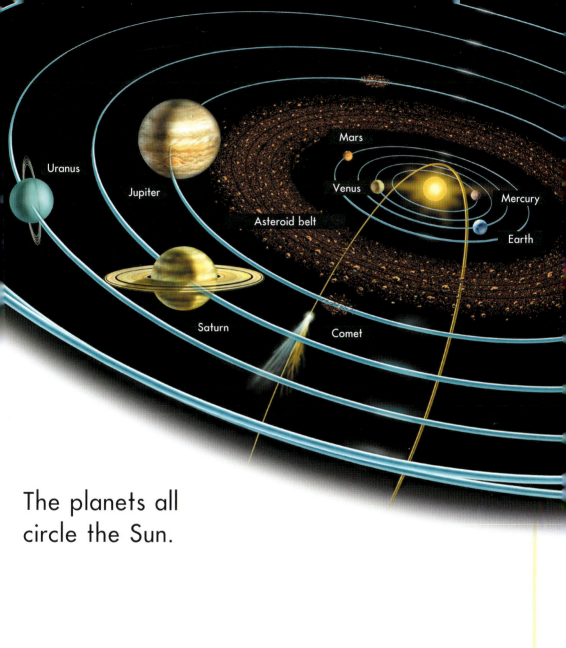

Uranus

Jupiter

Mars

Venus

Mercury

Asteroid belt

Earth

Saturn

Comet

The planets all
circle the Sun.

Glossary

meteor A piece of rock that falls to Earth from space.

planet Our solar system has nine planets that circle the Sun. The planets are called Mercury, Venus, Earth, Mars, Jupiter, Saturn, Uranus, Neptune and Pluto.

sunset The time at night when the Sun sets.

telescope A machine that we can look through that makes objects far away look closer.